Tropical Trees

OF HAWAI'I

By Paul Wood

Photography by
Ron Dahlquist

W9-BRY-062

ISLAND HERITAGE
PUBLISHING

ISLAND HERITAGE™
P U B L I S H I N G
A DIVISION OF THE MADDEN CORPORATION

94-411 KŌʻAKI STREET, WAIPAHU, HAWAIʻI 96797
Orders: (800) 468-2800 • Information: (808) 564-8800
Fax: (808) 564-8877
islandheritage.com

ISBN #: 0-93154-841-1
First Edition, First Printing, 2004

Photography by Ron Dahlquist
unless otherwise noted.

Contents

About This Book

In Hawai'i you'll sometimes see full-grown trees barreling down the highway at fifty miles an hour. They've been scooped out of the ground by a back-hoe and thrown onto a flatbed hauler with their roots hanging everywhere. People who know proper plant care—who know about cautious transplanting, about surgical ball-and-burlap handling of the undisturbed root core of only very young trees—these people know that you can't haul a tree, totally bare-root under highway conditions, and expect it to live. But the back-hoe driver knows from experience: "You put the buggah in the ground, it going grow."

Trees love Hawai'i even more than people do. Their leaves eat up the sunshine. Their roots dig into the porous lava rock. People have brought trees to the islands from all over the planet, and most of these species thrive. As a result, Hawai'i's tree-scape is extremely diverse—more diverse even than its human population—and this diversity gives daily life in the islands a subliminal beauty.

Some of these trees are tame—the tropical shade trees, flowering trees, and fruit trees that haven't escaped into the Hawaiian wilderness. Perhaps they lack the presence of a certain insect or bird required for pollination. Perhaps human selection and breeding have rendered them sterile. Perhaps they just can't compete in the open, or they haven't yet found their niche. Whatever the reason, these trees are only found in the backyards or street corners where they were planted.

Most of the trees in this book, though, are at least to some extent wild. These can be divided into several groups, depending on their habits and history. For example, you find fairly recent importations that have begun setting seed and wandering into open areas. Of these, some are welcome. (No one ever complains about the blue-blooming jacarandas that are

(LEFT) shower tree

5

seeding themselves along certain mountain roadsides.) But some are pests. (Weedy trees such as Christmas-berry and black wattle, almost as aggressive as bamboo, seize hillsides and pastures with ravenous enthusiasm.)

Other wild trees moved into Hawai'i's forests a hundred or more years ago and now seem to belong. Hikers trek happily beneath guava, mango, and ironwood trees, regarding them as native plants rather than imports that arrived about the same time as cattle and horses.

Early Polynesian settlers brought in their own favorite species more than a thousand years ago. Today, trees such as coconut, breadfruit, kukui, and mountain apple stand as defining features of the wild Hawaiian landscape, and few people think of them as anything other than true natives. But Hawai'i does have its true natives, endemic species that evolved in the islands without human assistance. Alas, of this last category we can show very few examples. Koa and 'ōhi'a are the most prominent of these endemic plants today. But most native species are rare and endangered, so they live beyond the scope of this common-tree guide.

Our purpose in this book is to help you identify the trees that you usually see as you travel around the Hawaiian islands. (Emphasis on "usually.") A small guide such as this cannot be comprehensive, so we have omitted some oddballs and rarities.

Oddballs are trees that simply don't belong in the tropics. For example, lots of trees require a northern-style winter chill. Even so, people who live on Hawai'i's higher slopes try to cultivate such things as apples, peaches, and plums. The fruit is always terrible, but the gardeners persist in the belief that everything grows in Paradise. Rarities are the trees you are likely to find only in Hawai'i's botanical gardens—the baobab, for example, with its freakish hollow trunk formerly used by African natives as a repository for poets and buffoons. Apples and baobabs are not common in Hawai'i; therefore they and their sort are not treated in this little book.

Other trees—lemons, for example, or magnolias—are so well known or so characteristic of other parts of the world that we left them out. We focused on plants that define the mixed look of today's Hawaiian tree-scape.

Given such a diversity of tree habitat and history, how is one to organize a simple guide of this sort? At first we considered grouping the trees by categories in the manner suggested above—natives, forest trees, backyard trees and so on. In Hawai'i, though, those divisions break down quickly. Trees are constantly escaping their fenced enclosures. And vice versa. The koa, for example, is an endemic species that's popular today as a home landscape feature. What's more, the division of trees by these categories would have blurred a more natural division that we decided to feature—the evolutionary relationship of trees by their plant families.

Certain families have been amazingly successful and generous in supplying Hawai'i with trees. The myrtle family, for example (Myrtaceae) includes an important endemic tree ('ōhi'a), a Polynesian introduction (mountain apple), and forest features with various histories (guava and eucalyptus, for example). The pea-and-bean family (Fabaceae) runs a similar gamut, everything from the endemic koa and wiliwili to backyard specimen plants such as bauhinia and the shower trees.

Our hope is that the family-based organization will provide you with pleasurable insights that will add to your enjoyment of these trees.

We have arranged these plant families in an order that is commonly accepted by botanists as representing the sequence of evolution—the more "primitive" types first, the more "advanced" (that is, more recently evolved) last. Thus, we begin with tree ferns and conifers because these types of plants are assumed to have been on earth prior to the evolution of flowering plants.

When a family contains more than one member, we list them alphabetically by genus name.

Scientific names do change from time to time as botanists learn more about different species and their relationships. Whenever possible, we have relied on the authority of Bishop Museum Press's two-volume *Manual of the Flowering Plants of Hawai'i* by Wagner, Herbst, and Sohmer. Our special mahalo to Pam Shingaki, at University of Hawai'i's Maui Agricultural Research Center, for reviewing this book's text and design.

We hope that the photographs, descriptions, and tidbits of natural science will inspire you to stop and notice—see, touch, smell, and value—these dignified citizens of the Hawaiian landscape, our beloved trees.

plumeria

A Brief History

Today about half of Hawai'i's total land surface can rightfully be called forest. But for many thousands of years—before humans arrived—trees blanketed the islands, growing on every slope, high and low, wet and dry. They dominated in a casual way, leaving room for the low-growing plants, the lichens, the spiders, snails and birds. These lesser creatures all lived and evolved in micro-worlds defined by the presence of tall timber. On wind-facing slopes, trees absorbed the blows of tropical storms. In dry areas, trees raked water out of the passing mists and provided canopies of protection from scorching sunlight. On every island's volcanic surface, trees did the major job of soil-making, cracking the lava with their deep-delving roots and mulching it with their fallen limbs.

Considering the origin of the Hawaiian islands—volcanic fire and molten rock bursting forth in the middle of the Pacific Ocean thousands of miles from any other land—it's a wonder that they bore trees or plants of any kind. The seeds of tree pioneers had to travel somehow, by floating, blowing, or hitching a ride, across impossible saltwater distances. Against all odds, though, about seventy-eight species of trees managed the journey and, over time, evolved into some three hundred tree types that are unique to Hawai'i.

Such an impossible journey looks a bit more possible when you consider the great expanse of time involved. Scientists estimate that the Hawaiian archipelago is somewhere between five and ten million years old. Therefore, the native trees that we know today could have resulted from the arrival of just one successful immigrant every sixty thousand to one hundred twenty thousand years.

When human beings arrived—and we think this happened less than two thousand years ago—the slow dominion of trees began to experience radical change. The early Polynesian settlers used slash-and-burn methods to

clear fields for agricultural uses.
Although they discovered innumer-
able uses for Hawai'i's endemic
trees—for tool-making, construction, dyes, medicines, and ornaments—they also introduced and
fostered their own favorites. Some
examples of these Polynesian introductions featured in this book are:
breadfruit, coconut, kukui, hau,
and 'ōhi'a 'ai or mountain apple.
Observations by the first Western
visitors, beginning with the arrival
of Captain Cook in 1778, indicate
that the Hawaiians had pushed the
tree-line about three miles back from the shore on all islands. These "dis-
coverers" also marveled at the extent of agricultural development, and
they praised the Hawaiians as the most industrious farmers in all the
Pacific. Clearly the Polynesians were succeeding in a slow war of conquest against the native forests.

breadfruit

With the arrival of the Western world, this conquest moved into high gear.
Between 1810 and 1820 the Hawaiian rulers ordered a direct attack, com-
manding commoners to lay down their farm tools and hike into the mountains to cut and haul the native sandalwood trees. In short order, the
kingdom killed and sold over thirty thousand tons of the sweet-smelling
timber, exhausting the forests of that resource. The kingdom used the profit
to pay down debt incurred from its indulgence in Western luxuries such as
furniture, rum, and fancy uniforms. Since then, thousands of acres of forest
have been converted to agricultural land and pasture, or they have been
degraded by the actions of invasive animals and weeds. Most of the original three hundred species have retreated to small, hard-to-access pockets
of endangered terrain. The losses have been especially severe in the dry-

land forest areas, which once supported the greatest diversity of Hawai'i's endemic tree species. Only about four percent of the original dryland forests now remain.

On a brighter note, Cook's discovery and the end of Hawai'i's isolation opened the floodgates of introduced tree species. Some of the introduced trees became established so early and so well that they now dominate certain forest types in the islands. These successful aliens include kiawe (mesquite), guava, and mango. Also, forestry efforts to establish timber crops or restore watershed areas have given the islands large stands of various types of eucalyptus and even some notable high-altitude man-made forests of mixed conifers—pines, cypresses, and redwoods. And it's fair to say that the most delightful shade and flowering trees of tropical regions—and many of temperate regions—from around the world all thrive in Hawai'i's yards, streets, and roadsides.

It's surprising to realize how much of what looks like natural forest in Hawai'i is actually the result of deliberate planting. The mountains behind Honolulu were bare only eighty years ago. The forest parks on the Volcano Road (Hawai'i island), the koa and silk oak trees of Kōke'e (Kaua'i), the eucalyptus of Makawao (Maui), and the jungle trees along Maui's famous road to Hāna —these are all largely planted. Much of this planting in the forest reserves was done in the 1930s as part of the Civilian Conservation Corps program, and it repaired quite a bit of the tree loss that the forests had suffered in the preceding century.

koa

Even so, Hawai'i has no timber industry. There have been various experiments in the past. For example, from 1909 to 1917 a large mill in Puna (Hawai'i island) cut railroad ties from the heavy, hard wood of the native 'ōhi'a lehua. But that mill, like the railroads, has vanished from island life. As recently as the late 1970s a chipping plant on that same island was shredding eucalyptus and shipping it to Japan for use as paper pulp. But the most viable and most admired wood industry in Hawai'i stems from the beauty of its hardwoods when treated as a fine-detail building material or as an art medium. The native koa is highly esteemed for its beauty as a cabinet wood. Many island craftspeople perpetuate the old Hawaiian skill of woodworking and bowl-making, turning out gorgeous calabashes from not only koa but also milo, mango, Norfolk pine, and many other trees illustrated in this book.

milo

Few places on earth have such a great diversity of topography and climate within such a small area. Hawai'i's tree habitats include sandy beaches, long sea cliffs, and deep canyons with knife-thin ridges. Three mountain peaks (Mauna Kea and Mauna Loa on Hawai'i island and Haleakalā on Maui) rise above timberline, which is about eight thousand feet. The island chain includes what is probably the wettest spot on Earth—Wai'ale'ale Peak on Kaua'i with a mean annual rainfall of four hundred sixty inches—and some barren lava flows that are rarely dampened. Thus, the number of habitats and niches for trees is very high. If human inhabitants choose to mālama 'āina—take care of the land—Hawai'i will always be a home for the Earth's most admirable trees.

(RIGHT) plumeria

The Trees

Tree Ferns

While not strictly "trees," certain trunked ferns are distinctive features of Hawai'i's tropical rainforests.

Dicksoniaceae

Cibotium chamissoi • **hāpu'u**

The largest native tree fern, found only in Hawai'i, hāpu'u is common in wet forests between eight hundred and six thousand feet elevation on all major islands. This is a characteristic understory plant in 'ōhi'a forests (see p. 88), and the best displays can be found on Hawai'i island in the forests of Puna, Hilo, and the Kohala Mountains. Giant fronds unroll from a densely hairy coil, and the rough leafstalks wear beards of stiff, shaggy hairs. This fern's unbranching trunk gets to ten feet high on the average. One giant in the Big Island's Hōnaunau Forest Reserve reached thirty-five feet high with a frond-spread of twenty-four feet. These are hardy plants that can withstand cattle damage. If uprooted by wild pigs, they will re-root themselves so long as the fiddle-head top is undamaged. During the 1960s the trunks or "poles" were harvested for use as an orchid-growing medium. "Pots" made of short cross sections are a mainstay of the vanda orchid industry.

Blechnaceae

Sadleria cyatheoides • 'ama'u

Hawai'i's most common trunked fern, 'ama'u grows in open lava flows and wet forests. It's not much of a tree, really—the slender unbranched trunk gets three to five feet high. However, a sixteen-footer was cut in the 1950s and displayed for many years at Hawaiian Fern-Wood Ltd. in Hilo. The soft, hair-like scales on the young leaves have been harvested commercially for stuffing mattresses and pillows. The Hawaiians used to beat the leaf stalks for sizing their kapa cloth, and they extracted a red dye from the outer trunk. They sometimes thatched their

homes with the fronds and laid them around their dryland crops as a mulch. In hard times they would bake the tasteless inner trunks for food. Halema'uma'u, the name of Kīlauea Volcano's fire pit, basically means the house of the 'ama'u fern. This old name attests to the strong presence of this fern in that habitat.

Cycadaceae

Botanists regard the cycads as living fossils. The family, with many now-extinct genera and species, flourished in earlier geological periods, especially the Mesozoic era. Many people believe that these were the first plants to escape the limitations of fern-style reproduction through spores—in other words, that they were the inventors of seeds. The invention of seeds led to the evolution of every tree that follows in this book.

Cycas circinalis • **cycad, Sago palm**

The cycad shown here, often called Sago palm, can get fifteen feet tall in Hawai'i. Its sturdy, ringed trunk culminates in rosettes of heavy, feather-shaped leaves that can grow as long as nine feet. New leaves form at the top in a ring, the whole set pushing out simultaneously to claim the next stage of growth. Male trees produce erect pollen-bearing cones about two feet long. Female trees

Paul Wood

make special woolly foot-long leaves that form seeds along their edges. Seeds are poisonous when raw, but people sometimes cook or bake them as a famine food. This particular cycad is native to the region stretching from India to the Philippines.

Araucariaceae

In parts of the world where conifers such as pine, fir, cypress, and cedar flourish, the related auracaria family is unknown. These conifers are confined to the southern Pacific region, with many species in New Caledonia. The fossil record shows, however, that araucarias once grew across the globe from Greenland to Antarctica. These plants are dioecious—in other words, some are male, some female. They are long-lived trees that grow up to two hundred feet tall. The indoor plant trade grows them as potted ornamentals because their amazing symmetry—five or so branches shooting horizontally from the same ring on the trunk—gives them an artificial-Christmas-tree look. In fact, Hawai'i residents will often avoid the high price of imported Christmas trees by chopping the araucaria in the backyard.

Araucaria columnaris • **Cook pine**

As Captain Cook and crew explored New Caledonia, they were the first Westerners to see what is now called Cook pine. At first they believed they were seeing columns of stone. Later they realized that these straight, narrow trees could be harvested and milled into masts, spars, and all sorts of timber. So early explorers carried them elsewhere in the Pacific, including Hawai'i, as a potential source of spare parts. A row of Cook pines planted along the summit ridge of Lāna'i adds significantly to that small island's water table by reaching into the moist air and sieving fog, drip by drop, to the soil below.

Araucaria heterophylla • **Norfolk Island pine**

Similar to Cook pine, especially when small, the Norfolk Island pine matures into a much wider, laxer tree. Its leaf scales are narrower and more numerous. This araucaria is probably more widely grown in Hawai'i than any other, but the seed and seedlings are often confused with other species.

Other Conifers

pine, redwood, cypress

Although there are no conifers native to Hawai'i, many species of the most common cone-bearing trees have been planted, not only in home gardens but also in upper-elevation forest reserves such as this one on Maui, the Kula Forest Reserve at Poli Poli Springs. Conifers represented here include several types of pine (*Pinus* sp.), cypress (*Cupressus* sp.), and two members of the redwood family (*Taxodiaceae*) – the sugi (*Cryptomeria japonica*) of Japan and China, and the Pacific Coast redwood (*Sequoia sempervirens*).

Poli Poli forest

Cupressus sempervirens • Italian cypress

Italian cypress is popular as an ornamental plant, carrying as it does the formal, classical feeling of ancient Greece and Rome. The champion is identified to be at 'Ulupalakua Ranch on Maui—height eighty-two feet with a spread of twenty feet.

Pandanaceae

This antique family was once widespread on the planet, but it is now restricted to the Pacific-basin tropics. Family traits include roots that protrude from trunk and branch, a spiraling growth habit, and the sexual distinction of male and female plants.

Pandanus tectorius • **hala**

Hala, also called screwpine, is common throughout the Hawaiian islands in coastal areas, especially on windward slopes from sea level to about two thousand feet. Hala can be recognized at a glance for its unique prop roots that buttress its smooth, light gray trunks. Stout, widely forking branches end in spirally arranged leaf clusters; leaves are large and strap-shaped with saw-tooth edges. Male flowers are tiny and fragrant, crowded into drooping clusters one to two feet long. Female flowers form a large ball-shaped fruit that looks something like a pineapple or pine cone. Male trunks are hard and solid throughout; female trunks are soft and fibrous within. Hollowed out, this female wood has been used as water pipes. Hala leaves (lau hala) served many purposes for the native Hawaiians, who plaited them into baskets, mats, hats, and sandals. A roof thatched with lau hala would last up to fifteen years, compared with only three years for coconut leaves. The fruit served as a famine food but was generally used as a lei feature, also broken down for small "brushes" used to apply coloring to kapa cloth.

Poaceae

The grass family, one of the largest plant groups, has abandoned the woody stem structure that makes for true trees. Certain bamboos, however, rise to tree-like heights.

Bambusa vulgaris • **common bamboo, 'ohe**

Grass family traits can be recognized in bamboo's hollow, jointed stems and papery, linear leaves. It's a natural marvel that this grass reaches heights of fifty feet. The 'ohe was introduced to Hawai'i from China in the early nineteenth century, and native people quickly adopted it for use in making fishing poles and canoe outriggers. The young shoots, boiled, are eaten by all ethnic groups in the islands. (Prior to discovery, the Hawaiians had already introduced another type of bamboo, *Schizostachyum glaucifolium*, which they used to fashion knives, fans, mats, bellows, and musical instruments such as

the nose flute.) One can see enormous stands of 'ohe on O'ahu in Nu'uanu Valley near Reservoir No. 3 and along Maui's road to Hāna. These mini-forests are actually interlocked clones of single, individual plantings. After many years of growth, these bamboo stands will bloom simultaneously, produce seed, and then die.

24

Palmaceae

Dozens of palms have been introduced to Hawai'i as ornamentals. To list them all would surpass the scope of this book. The palm family is an ancient tropical group, with most of roughly two thousand six hundred members coming from the Indo-Malaya region. Only one type of palm came to Hawai'i without human help—the loulu (genus *Pritchardia*). At least nineteen types of loulu evolved in the islands; they are hard to find, many endangered.

Cocos nucifera • **coconut, niu**

This familiar symbol of the tropics is ranked among the ten most useful tree species in the world. The fruit provides a nutritious, pure beverage and a sweet flesh that can be eaten from the "spoon meat" stage (young and soft) to full maturity (hard and dense). The dry mature pulp, called copra, yields the coconut oil used in lotions and cooking. The Hawaiians, who apparently brought coconut to the islands, planted and managed groves of these trees, which can reach up to one hundred feet tall. They used the oil for lamp fuel, ointment, and hair tonic, the leaves for thatching and weaving, and the fibers from leaf-bases and fruit husks to make cordage of various kinds, sandals, strainers, and

25

sennit for house construction. Coconut husks—natural bowls—make useful utensils. The sweet sap of coconut flower buds has been used to make sugar, wine, vinegar, and (through the action of bees) honey. The coconut fruit is one of the largest seeds known, surpassed only by the "double coconut" of the Seychelles Islands (*Lodoicea maldivica*, which can be seen at Foster Garden). Seeds can germinate after floating in salt water for months.

This was the official tree of the Territory of Hawai'i, before statehood.

Mascarena lagenicaulis • **bottle palm**
Roystonea regia • **royal palm**

bottle palm

(ABOVE) fruit on palm
(RIGHT) royal palm

Agavaceae

Certain relatives of the lily, the tulip, and the iris (monocots) adopted the size, strength, and to some extent the woodiness of true trees (dicots). In the agave family you find botanical giants such as the century plant and the yucca, six endemic Hawaiian species in the genus *Pleomele*, and the beloved Hawaiian ti plant. The dracaenas are close relatives of these.

Dracaena draco • **dragon tree**

In the Canary Islands, its homeland, the dragon tree attains great height and age, with crowds of sword-like, two-foot-long leaves on the tips of thick, stubby branches. Specimens of great stature are unusual in Hawai'i. Perhaps we just need to wait another century or so. The dried sap, called "Dragon's Blood," makes a good varnish for fine furniture.

28

Musaceae

Though none of the tropical plants in the family of the banana can rightly call itself a tree, most of them grow with tremendous vertical enthusiasm.

Musa x paradisiaca • **banana**

Banana is one of the great food plants of the tropics. From ancient times humans have hybridized and crossed this plant so often that no one can now explain its botanical history. The Hawaiians themselves developed seventy different varieties for their own uses, then forbade the eating of bananas by women, under pain of death. Among the many curiosities of the banana is the fact that it is not a tree at all (even though some varieties grow thirty feet tall). The "trunks" are made of leaf-stems that clasp together as a stalk, rather like celery. This clasped stalk is so tight and so heavy with water that new leaves, which push up from below through the center of the trunk, must produce a kind of talcum powder to smooth their passage. After a year or more of rapid growth, the banana stalk receives a flower spear, also pushed up from

below. This spear emerges at the crown, then turns and hangs, developing a massive column of the familiar banana "hands." Once

the fruit ripens, the whole "tree" must be cut down, or else left to rot and wither. In the meantime, the core of the plant, an underground corm, has been busy sending up suckers as replacements. Hawaiians call these new generations "keiki" or children.

a rare variegated banana variety

Strelitziaceae

Bird-of-paradise is the mostly widely known member of this small African family. Some botanists place this entire group in the banana family, then add the heliconias, too. The point is that the banana and the travelers palm are similar in many ways.

Ravenala madagascariensis • **travelers palm**

This odd plant from Madagascar combines a palm-like trunk with banana-like leaves, then adds a trick of its own—flatness. All the leaves fan out along a single plane, forming an arch of wind-tattered greenery. New leaves grow up the center, eventually moving to the outside where they droop and fall. Travelers palm leaves are among the largest to be found on Earth, growing up to nine feet long on even longer stems. At the base of each stem, a closed cavity holds a quart or more of water. This water reservoir (according to one theory) helps support the huge leaves in strong winds. It is also available to quench the thirst of savvy travelers—hence the plant's common name. Flowers push out from the leaf-crotches, looking like giant green-and-white bird-of-paradise flowers. A popular ornamental plant in Hawai'i, travelers palm grows quickly to thirty feet tall.

Casuarinaceae

This unique family has just one genus and only about fifty species. Most are native to Australia.

Casuarina glauca • **casuarina, ironwood**

Eleven species of casuarina have been introduced to Hawai'i for forestry purposes. Locally, for some reason, people call them all "ironwood." Other common names: beefwood, she-oak (the wood being similar to oak but not as strong), and Australian pine (it is not a pine, nor even a conifer). These are evergreen trees recognizable for their many drooping slender green twigs that look like pine needles. Whereas pine needles are true leaves, the "needles" of casuarina are actually twigs that, being green, do the work of photosynthesis. Close inspection of the twigs reveals many joints decorated with gray or brown scales. These scales are the much-diminished leaves. Casuarinas bear separate male and female flowers, usually on the same tree. Female flowers produce round, hard, cone-like fruits. Ironwoods thrive on depleted, eroded land. Like the legumes, they are able to fix nitrogen—that is, replenish soil fertility through a symbiotic relationship with a fungus that finds shelter in the roots. *Casuarina glauca* is the most common species of ironwood in Hawai'i. Its habit of sending up root-shoots and suckers makes it ideal for the primary planting purpose—recapturing erosion scars. The same trait makes it a running pest in some areas.

Moraceae

The mulberry family has one thousand species and is widespread in tropical and subtropical regions. It includes many plants of great human value—for instance, the edible mulberry (whose leaves are fed to silkworms), figs, the wauke or paper mulberry (*Broussonetia papyrifera*) cultivated by the Hawaiians as the bark source for their kapa cloth, the controversial weed *Cannabis sativa*, and the trees pictured below.

Artocarpus altilis • **breadfruit, 'ulu**

This handsome, sturdy tree deserves to be planted simply for the enjoyment of its beauty. The rich green leaves are deeply lobed and almost two feet long. The Polynesians brought this tree to Hawai'i for its fruit—a dense, lumpy-skinned sphere up to eight inches across—that consists almost entirely of a cream-colored, starchy pulp. Picked green, then roasted or boiled, the fruit provides great quantities of rather tasteless nutrition. Hawaiians didn't eat much breadfruit, mostly using it to fatten hogs. However, 'ulu poi is still prized—breadfruit pounded with taro. In the Marquesas breadfruit is still the primary foodstuff. There, it is mashed and fermented into a cheese-like substance, then eaten with a sauce of coconut milk, seawater, and lime juice. The wood is so light that the Hawaiians used it for surfboards. Some say that breadfruit wood was the preferred construction material for the decking that tied together the hulls of the great double-hulled voyaging canoes. Broken twigs exude a milky juice or latex. According to tradition, bird-catchers used this sticky stuff, smeared on branches, to catch the feet of forest birds. Bird-catchers would then climb the trees, pluck the few brightest feathers (to be woven into the spectacular feather cloaks of the chiefs), then clean the birds' feet and release them.

In 1789 the British government sent Captain William Bligh (formerly of Cook's expedition) to transport potted breadfruit trees from Tahiti to the West Indies, estimating that three or four trees would sustain a slave laborer for a year. The trip turned out poorly, though it provided the Hollywood-scale plot for *Mutiny on the Bounty*. Bligh survived the mutiny and completed his agricultural task in 1793.

Artocarpus heterophyllus • **jack fruit**

The jack fruit is not common in Hawai'i. But if you see one, you will wonder about the huge green blobs hanging from its bark. These knobby sculptures are actually some of the largest fruits known on Earth—up to three feet long and forty pounds heavy. No wonder they need such woody support—trunks, large branches, even roots underground. When ripe, the fruit has an unpleasant smell but a sweet or tangy white pulp that is eaten raw or cooked. The big seeds are roasted like chestnuts. Trees can be fifty feet tall, with oblong leaves about six inches long.

figs and banyans

Ficus, the fig genus of the family Moraceae with its eight hundred species, is one of the most robust groups in the plant kingdom—full of wide-spreading, earth-conquering trees that pump out great quantities of fruit. The group lives by an ingenious mode of reproduction. Flowers form inside a globular capsule, completely hidden from the world except for a small hole at the end of the sphere. Tiny wasps hatch in there with the flowers; the males are wingless and never leave. The females mate, then exit through the hole dusted with pollen. They find another fruit, slip inside scattering pollen, then lay their eggs and expire. Each type of

Ficus practices this symbiosis with its own unique species of fig wasp.

About sixty kinds of *Ficus* have come to Hawai'i, but only four fig wasps have been introduced. The edible fig, so important to the life and lore of the Mediterranean region, does grow in Hawai'i but not with great success.

Ficus carica • edible fig

Ficus benghalensis • **Indian banyan**

The Indian banyan is one of the broadest-spreading of all trees. A single individual in Kea'au Village, Puna, has a diameter of one hundred ninety-five feet. The well-known banyan at the town center of Lahaina, Maui, covers three-quarters of an acre. Banyans achieve this impossible spread by dropping aerial roots from the underside of their branches. These aerial roots dangle like wires until they touch the ground, at which point they grow into the earth and fatten into subsidiary trunks. Native to India, this banyan is sacred to the Hindus.

Ficus elastica • **rubber tree**

In colder climates, people know the rubber tree as a popular indoor potted plant. In Hawai'i, planted in the ground, *Ficus elastica* shows its affinity with the banyans, growing aggressively to one hundred feet tall and dropping aerial roots from the trunk and limbs. The stiff, oval

leaves get over a foot long. In some parts of the world this native of India is tapped for its milky sap, which turns into an elastic substance similar to rubber. Horticultural varieties include "decora," with shiny attractive leaves, and "variegata," with white or cream colorations.

Ficus microcarpa • **Chinese banyan**

The fig wasp for the Chinese banyan was introduced to Hawai'i in 1938. Birds harvest the fruit and disperse the seeds wherever they go. As a result, you find this banyan sprouting in unlikely places—in the crack of a wall or on the branch of another tree. The aerial roots slowly put a strangle hold on the host structure, widening and eventually swallowing whatever gave the tree its start in life. Regardless of its parasitic habit, this is a handsome evergreen tree smaller in stature and leaf size than its Indian cousin.

Proteaceae

The protea family is best known in Hawai'i for a flower-farm crop—the spectacular protea flowers. These bloom on shrubs native to South Africa and Australia.

Grevillea robusta • **silk oak**

This handsome Australian tree has been widely planted for shade, ornament, and reforestation—and it has escaped to become a bit of a weedy pest in certain areas. Leaves are ferny-looking, dark green above and silvery with silky hairs below. Flowers are golden and brilliant in April and May. Bark is light gray, rough and thick with many deep furrows. The pink-brown wood is excellent for machining; however, the sawdust causes der-

matitis in some people. Silk oak was first planted in Hawai'i in about 1880, used as a shade and street tree, and is still (according to one estimation) the second-most commonly planted tree in the state.

Macadamia integrifolia • **macadamia**

The macadamia nut was first planted in Hawai'i in 1890, brought from subtropical eastern Australia. The land "down under" is home to many members of the protea family, including this dark, handsome tree. Leaves are thin, about six inches long, and edged with sharp teeth. Small white flowers emerge on tassels, then slowly develop into a bountiful fall crop of hard, dense nuts. The nuts involve a leathery, two-valved case roughly one inch across enclosing a round, shiny brown shell that must be cracked with a hammer blow. The nutritious white kernel has become a minor industry in Hawai'i, especially on the Big Island. About seventy percent fat, these kernels contain vitamin B1, calcium, phosphorus, and iron.

Polygonaceae

The buckwheat family consists mostly of herbs that thrive in temperate regions. The following tree of the tropics stands as an exception.

Coccoloba uvifera • **sea grape**

This small tree is planted along sandy beaches as an ornamental and windbreak. The thick, round, somewhat kidney-shaped leaves (slightly broader than long) are easily recognizable, as are the grape-like clusters of purple (edible) fruits. The smooth gray bark peels off the trunks in small flakes. Older leaves redden. Fruit can be eaten raw or made into jelly or wine. Rolled in cones of paper, the fruit is sold on the street in tropical America, its native habitat.

Annonaceae

The custard-apple family includes about six hundred species of tropical shrubs and trees cultivated for their fruit and for their perfume (the ylang-ylang from India, for example).

Annona cherimola • **cherimoya**

Cherimoya is a small tree—no more than twenty-five feet high—with oval, velvety leaves. The fruit is the same color as the leaves, medium green, and shaped like a heart, with slight depressions at every square defined by its cross-hatched surface. Inside the fruit, cream-white pulp yields a delicious, somewhat acidic juice. People call this the "ice cream fruit." Its flavor is a blend of pineapple, mango, and strawberry. This fruit tree originated in the jungle valleys of Bolivia, Colombia, and Ecuador; botany pioneers brought it to Hawai'i in 1890. Fruits are picked full-grown but still hard. After they turn yellow-green and soft, people eat them out of hand or scooped with a spoon. The hard seeds have medicinal and even toxic qualities.

Lauraceae

A tree-like family of South America and southeastern Asia, the laurels include two of Hawai'i's native plants.

Cinnamomum camphora • **camphor**

Classically shaped and visually pleasing, the camphor tree forms a dense, rounded crown of shiny green leaves. These leaves are just three or four inches long, tapering to a long point at the apex. The entire tree carries the spicy aroma of camphor, readily perceived by crushing some of the foliage. The yellow-brown wood is also strongly scented. For this reason, and because the soft wood is fine textured and takes a good polish, cabinetmakers sometimes work it into chests and closet linings. The odor works as an insect repellent. Steam distillation of the leaves and wood yields the camphor gum and oil of medicine and commerce. Trees grow to about eighty feet tall and form a hefty trunk with a gray, furrowed bark. A native of tropical Asia (including Vietnam, Taiwan, and Japan), camphor has naturalized now not only in Hawai'i but also in the southern US along the Gulf coast and in California.

Paul Wood

Persea americana • **avocado**

Avocado, a close relative of the camphor, first came to Hawai'i in the early nineteenth century. By 1910 it was one of the most common trees in lowland gardens. The US Division of Forestry has planted thousands of avocado trees in the forest reserves on all Hawaiian islands, and the trees adapt well to wild living. Most avocados flower in early spring—the flowers are minute but so abundant they seem to cover the tree—and bear fruit from June to August. However,

there are so many varieties in the islands now that you can find the fruit all year round. The University of Hawai'i has developed numerous varieties that are superior to US mainland varieties in flavor, size, and production.

A medium-size tree, avocados grow to thirty feet tall, rarely to as big as sixty feet. The seven-inch-long, dark green leaves, aromatic when crushed, form a thick, dense canopy. There's no need to describe this tree's buttery green fruit, which is as nutritious as it is popular. Avocado is native to Mexico, Guatemala, and Honduras.

Rosaceae

The rose family, so famous in regions colder than Hawai'i, includes the apple, the pear, the plum, the peach, the apricot, and so on. Few of these plants live well in tropical Hawai'i. However, strawberries and blackberries have managed to escape, and Hawai'i has two native species of *Rubus*, the prickly-stemmed blackberry/raspberry genus.

Eriobotrya japonica • **loquat**

Loquat is a low, evergreen, drought-resistant tree from central China. The dark leaves are hard, up to ten inches long, pointed at both ends, toothed along the edges, shiny above, and rusty-woolly below. The small white fragrant flowers crowd the branch tips in rusty clusters each fall. In the winter, loquats produce juicy yellow fruits one or two inches long. Loquat fruit is something like a large-seeded pear. Good varieties are packed with flavor. In Hawai'i, these trees do best at elevations of three thousand to five thousand feet.

Fabaceae

The legume or pea-and-bean family is enormously successful and varied—the third-largest group of all the flowering plants. Many members enrich the earth on which they grow by pulling nitrogen out of the air and fixing it in the soil, where it serves as natural fertilizer. The family includes many important food and fodder plants. For our present purposes, though, Fabaceae deserves praise for producing the most distinctive specimen and flowering trees of the Hawaiian landscape.

Acacia koa • **koa**

The koa is Hawai'i's largest and most common native tree. It is also one of the few endemic plants used routinely in landscape plantings. These are fast-growing trees that can reach heights of one hundred feet. The tell-at-a-glance feature is the unique foliage—flat and sickle-shaped. Curiously, these "leaves" are actually modified leafstalks (petioles, to use the proper term). Koa's true leaves—when you can spot them on the growing tips of young twigs—are much-divided and "ferny," like the leaves of all other acacias. Koa is prized for its beautiful reddish-brown wood, which has a weight and strength comparable to black walnut and polishes to a golden luster.

Hawaiians used koa for house timbers, canoes, and paddles. Cabinetworkers turn the wood into bowls, furniture, and interior paneling. Today koa canoes are the pride of many an outrigger canoe club. But logs suitable for such large artifacts have become extremely scarce.

Acacia mearnsii • **wattle, black-wattle acacia**

A close relative of the koa, the wattle tree does not share its cousin's good reputation. During the 1930s the Division of Forestry planted this Australian native by the thousands on Oʻahu, Maui, and Hawaiʻi. Now it is considered a noxious weed, as it quickly transforms pastureland into reedy, gray, lifeless forests. This effect can be glimpsed especially from the roadside in Maui's Kula district. Leaves, up to six inches long, are finely divided and feather-like. Bark is gray to brown and fairly smooth. The tree is not used in Hawaiʻi, except as a decent firewood.

Bauhinia monandra • **pink bauhinia, St. Thomas tree**
Bauhinia blakeana • **Hong Kong orchid tree**

Leaves shaped like butterfly wings—two wing-like lobes joined at the stem—identify several types of bauhinia that are grown in Hawai'i as small ornamental trees. Flowers in orchid-like colors of purple, rose, and white grace these ornamentals each spring.

(LEFT) pink bauhinia
(ABOVE) Hong Kong orchid tree

Paul Wood

Paul Wood

52

Cassia spp. • **shower trees**

Arguably the most gorgeous flowering trees in Hawai'i are those readily grouped under the common name "shower trees." These are small trees that, when not flowering, look like typical bean trees—fern-like subdivided leaves on gnarly, twiggy armature with an umbrella-like spread and usually decorated with hard, dark bean pods that hang from the stems. But each summer the shower trees bloom into clouds of fluffy color, floating masses of pink and/or gold that persist for several months.

Cassia fistula
- **golden shower**
native of India

Cassia javanica
- **pink-and-white shower**
native of Java and Sumatra

Cassia javanica x fistula
- **rainbow shower**

Cassia grandis
- **pink shower**
native of tropical America

Delonix regia • **royal poinciana**

For a few months in winter these small, gnarled, parasol-shaped trees stand bare, their fern-frond leaves having dropped to the ground. But in early spring they blaze into color—crimson, scarlet, and orange with touches of yellow. The show persists until leaf-drop time comes again, some nine months later. The flat, woody beanpods, more than a foot long, hang from the tree year-round, gradually turning from green to black. The narrow seeds are strung into lei. A native of Madagascar, the royal poinciana is one of the most beloved flowering trees in Hawai'i.

Erythrina sandwicense • **wiliwili**

At one time this small, gnarly native tree covered the lowland slopes on the dry sides of all Hawaiian islands. Now it has been largely replaced by introduced kiawe (*Prosopis pallida*, see page 62). Endemic to Hawai'i, wiliwili is a deciduous tree that produces showy displays of (usually) orange flowers from spring to July, during which time the trees are leafless. These flowers have the "sweet pea" design so characteristic of this family. Trees have stout, crooked trunks and reach heights of fifteen to thirty feet, spreading wider. The bark is light to reddish brown and is studded with stout spines. Leaves consist of three roundly triangular leaflets. This plant produces bright red beans, which the Hawaiians strung to make lei; Captain James Cook was given these lei when he made his fatal visit in 1778. You can see wiliwili on Maui while driving the leeward side of Haleakalā from 'Ulupalakua to Kaupō, and on Hawai'i island in the dry forest near Pu'uwa'awa'a. This native deserves to be more widely planted, as it propagates readily and thrives where others cannot.

Erythrina spp. • **coral trees, wiliwili**

Erythrina variegata var. orientalis
• tiger's claw, wiliwili haole

Several other species of *Erythrina* have been introduced as ornamentals in Hawai'i, particularly for their showy displays of orange-red flowers and their ability to withstand the tough conditions along roadsides and in parking lots. Elsewhere, people call these *Erythrina* types "coraltree" or "coralbean"; however, in the islands they are all called "wiliwili."

Pithecellobium dulce • **'opiuma**

This tough little tree was introduced about 1870 to provide some shade in the denuded, dry lowlands. The species makes a good highway and street tree in dry areas because it endures drought, heat, and shade. Leaves consist of four oblong leaflets with a pair of sharp spines at the base of each leaf-stem. Fruits are lumpy, dry

bean-pods that coil and curve on themselves. The black seeds come encased in a white edible pulp, sweet and tart, that can be made into a fruit drink. The seeds themselves are strung in lei. (Their similarity to seeds of opium poppy provoked the Hawaiian name "'opiuma.") This native of Mexico's Sonora Desert is employed for rough construction (posts, crates), for the tannin in its bark, and for a yellow dye it yields. The brown gum that oozes from its trunk can be dissolved to make a mucilage-like glue.

Pithecellobium saman • **monkeypod**

A magnificent shade tree, monkey-pod forms a dense umbrella of great width. The foot-long leaves, subdivided into inch-long leaflets, fold closed in the manner of butterfly wings at night and in cloudy weather. Each spring the trees drop their leaves altogether and remain bare for a few weeks. Monkeypod blooms from April to August, sending out clusters of pink and white

puffs, each one a bundle of wiry stamens. The fruit is a brown bean pod up to eight inches long that stays shut around a sticky, slightly sweet, licorice-flavored pulp. These trees, native to tropical America, arrived in Hawai'i in 1847—two seeds in the pocket of the king-dom's consul to Mexico City. One seedling came to dominate the corner of Bishop and Hotel Streets for fifty years. The other produced a grove of offspring at Kōloa, Kaua'i. Hawai'i's trade in souvenir carved bowls, which began in 1946, relies entirely on the golden brown wood of monkeypod. These bowls reflect the historic wood-working skills of the pre-monkeypod Hawaiians. (Never mind the fact that they are machine-made now in the Philippines, Thailand, or Malaysia.) For people of Hawai'i these are shade trees, not timber. The horizontal branches of one individual in O'ahu's Moanalua Gardens cover three-fourths of an acre.

Prosopis pallida • **kiawe**

Elsewhere, this New-World native is known as "mesquite"; in Hawai'i, it's "kiawe" (pronounced kee-ah-vay). In 1828 a Roman Catholic missionary named Father Alexis Bachelot planted Hawai'i's first specimen on the grounds of the new Catholic Mission in Honolulu. The seed came from a Peruvian tree growing in the French royal garden in Paris. By 1840 kiawe was a common shade tree in Honolulu, a previously tree-less town. From there it spread to all dry, flat coastal areas, bringing life to about ninety thousand acres

of barren soil—sand, clay, and lava. Fallen twigs are usually armed with wicked thorns. People say that the missionaries kept planting kiawe to force the natives to wear shoes. Such a claim ignores the vigor and value of the plants themselves. Setting aside its tendency to puncture, kiawe ranks among the most useful of all trees introduced to Hawai'i. The narrow yellow beanlike pods and the finely divided dull green leaves make excellent livestock feed. When honeybees were introduced in 1857, Hawai'i began exporting two hundred tons of kiawe honey a year. The wood is dark red-brown, extremely hard, and resistant to decay. People harvest and sell it for fence-posts, charcoal, and fuel.

When island people prepare a lū'au, this is the universally acknowledged proper firewood for the imu (the earth oven used for roasting pig).

Tamarindus indica • **tamarind**

Tamarind grows well at dry sea level in Hawai'i, where it forms an attractive shade tree with feathery blue-green foliage and rather showy yellow flowers. Its wood is dense and durable, useful for making chopping blocks and tool handles, or for burning a very hot fire. But the true and singular attraction of this tree is its fruit—a brittle-skinned beanpod packed with a sticky, brown, super-tart pulp. Throughout the tropics people use this flavorful goo to make a lemonade-like beverage, to create candy and preserves, and to season meats. In some parts of the world, the young leaves and flowers are eaten. Its flowers are also an important source of honey.

Paul Wood

Introduced to Hawai'i in 1797, tamarind was a popular town tree during the 1800s. Now that we live in the era of sidewalks and asphalt, this tree has lost popularity. Its abundant fruit drops to the paving and sticks there like chewing gum.

Paul Wood

Euphorbiaceae

The spurge family, a resourceful group of more than seven thousand species, ranges in expression from flat-growing weeds to showy shrubs (poinsettia and croton, for example) and some trees—one of which has great importance in Hawai'i.

Aleurites moluccana • **candlenut, kukui**

In 1959, the year of statehood, Hawai'i's legislature adopted the kukui as the state's official tree because of "its multiplicity of uses to the ancient Hawaiians for light, fuel, medicine, dye, and ornament, as well as the distinctive beauty of its light-green foliage." The silver-white flash of kukui is a common sight in Hawai'i's wet forests below about two thousand feet elevation, especially in the deepest parts of ravines. Leaves are broad and somewhat maple-like with three to five lobes (or they can be lobeless). Flowers, small and white, appear in terminal clusters. The fruit—that is, the kukui nut—provides the great utility of this plant. It forms like a walnut, surrounded by a

leathery flesh. The dense, hard nuts—white when immature, black later—are loaded with oil. They polish to a sheen. Unbroken, they are strung into lei and made into costume jewelry. The Hawaiians roasted and split them, then strung the seeds on a piece of coconut midvein and burned them for candlelight. They crushed the seeds to extract the oil, which they burned in simple stone lamps. (For a time, Hawai'i exported this oil for use in paints, varnishes, and medicines at the rate of ten thousand gallons a year. The oil is excellent for the skin and useful for clearing up stretch marks.) The Hawaiians also ate, and still eat, the roasted seeds, mixed with seaweed and salt, as a condiment called 'inamona—tasty, but when overindulged quite laxative. They used kukui's sap to waterproof their kapa cloth, the rind of its fruit to extract a dye for tattooing, and the bark of its roots for another dye to paint their canoes. For these and other labor-intensive reasons the early Polynesians brought kukui with them in their voyaging canoes. That's right—the Hawai'i state tree is not a native but a Malaysian plant favored by voyaging humans throughout the Pacific.

Anacardiaceae

The mango family includes the cashew nut and the pistachio, both of which are grown in Hawai'i but not commonly seen.

Mangifera indica • **mango**

The mango fruit, egg-shaped with its thin, sunset-colored skin, its juicy golden-orange flesh, and its single lens-shaped seed, provides sensual satisfaction matched by no other tropical food. Hawai'i's people favor three horticultural varieties with large, sweet fruit—the Pirie, the Hayden, and the Shibata. They also make use of the small, abundant fruit of the wild-growing "common mango"—old-timers use pole baskets to harvest them green, then pickle them with red food coloring. Fruit or no fruit, mango has become one of the most significant trees in the Hawaiian landscape. Introduced prior to 1825, mango established itself robustly in the lowland forests, and it towers over nearly every old home-site in the state. Trees have stout trunks and dense, dark, massive crowns of foot-long, lance-shaped leaves. New growth is copper-red. Flower-

clusters form a haze of activity over the trees in winter to spring, and fruits hang on long stalks six months later. The hard wood is prized for all sorts of quality craft purposes. It is blond, often mottled with dark spots and curious figuring. Mango is also one of Hawai'i's most important honey sources. Some people have a skin sensitivity to the fruit-peel, leaves, and sap of

mango, something like the rash caused by poison ivy and poison oak (which are members of the same family).

Schinus molle • **pepper tree**

This medium-size evergreen tree, native to dry areas of tropical America, has found its place as a popular ornamental in California and in Hawai'i. The pepper tree has a pleasant, soft, cascading look. Its slender branches hang, dangling much-divided leaves up to ten inches long. The leaves and fruit are loaded with fragrant, peppery oil. Individual trees are usually

either male or female. Female trees produce a distinctive fruit—clusters of small rosy globes, each one containing one peppercorn-like seed within a papery cover. This is not the true pepper of the spice trade, but it is sometimes ground and used to the same effect.

Schinus terebinthifolia • **Christmas-berry**

Despite its merry common name—inspired by the plant's winter displays of pellet-size red berries—the Christmas-berry is a pest, a landscape-devouring weed. It's a small, gnarly tree that grows up to twenty-five feet high and prefers to grow crown-to-crown, choking out all life below. The wood is useless even as firewood, perhaps only valuable as chipped mulch. Seeds are poisonous and the sap causes dermatitis. Fruiting branches, however, look right in a tropical yule wreath.

Sapindaceae

The soapberry family of tropical regions includes about two thousand species, four of which are Hawai'i natives.

Filicium decipiens • **fern tree**

People in Hawai'i grow this medium-size evergreen tree for ornamental reasons, specifically for its handsome fern-like foliage. The leaves, composed of twelve to sixteen narrow, stemless leaflets, make attractive additions to floral arrangements and are often cut and sold for that purpose. Native to India, the fern tree bears numerous small flowers that cluster in the leaf axils, eventually turning into oval, purple fruits about a half inch long.

Litchi chinensis • **litchi, lychee**

The litchi is a medium-size tree that forms a round, dense crown of shiny, drooping leaflets. These are oblong, pointed, three to seven inches long, and pale green when new. The petal-less flowers are obscure, but the fruit that results is unique and highly prized. This fruit consists of a lumpy, leathery red shell surrounding an opalescent, juicy meat. The large brown seeds slip easily away from the meat. People eat this delicious fruit fresh, canned, or dried into raisin-like "litchi nuts."

In Hawai'i you sometimes find a similar and related tree, the longan (*Euphoria longan*). Both trees originated in southern China. Longan is more robust than litchi, with smaller, blunter leaves, woolly brown twigs, and a copper-red color to the new growth. The fruit is similar to litchi but not so red on the outside and not as flavorful within.

Allan Seiden

Malvaceae

This family is most famous for its shrubs—hibiscus, for example, and cotton—and for garden plants such as okra and hollyhock. But at least two tree members hold honored places in the old flora of Hawai'i.

Hibiscus tileaceus • **hau**

This common shoreline tree tends to sprawl all over itself, building massive piles of prostrate limbs. Flowers are classic hibiscus—five big petals with a central pistil-stamen spike. They open yellow with a dark red eye-spot, then they darken—orange, red—then fall to the ground whole. Leaves are heart-shaped, up to five inches across, borne on long leaf-stems with seven to nine major veins radiating out from the base. Hau is

common to all Pacific seashores. Perhaps it drifted to Hawai'i by luck; perhaps it was brought by the Polynesians. The Hawaiians cut its soft, porous wood into canoe outriggers, fish-net floats, game spears, and kite sticks. They fashioned ropes and cords from its tough inner bark. They made fire by rubbing hardwood sticks against this receptive material; Hawai'i's Boy Scouts today earn merit badges for the same trick.

Thespesia populnea • **milo**

Milo is a common shoreline tree throughout the Pacific and has naturalized in the American tropics. Its tightly-sealed fruits—gray, pentagonal flattened capsules just over an inch in diameter—can float in saltwater for over a year and still sprout. This is a bright green, medium-size tree with yellow hibiscus-like flowers. Probably introduced by the Polynesians, milo is now common on Hawai'i shorelines and is planted as an ornamental shade tree. The wood is superb for craftwork. Sapwood is light brown, and

heartwood is red to chocolate in color. The Hawaiians carved it into beautiful calabashes. Contemporary wood-turners still do.

Sterculiaceae

The cocoa family is a tropical group of some seven hundred fifty species, most of them shrubby with soft wood. The most famous family member yields the core ingredient for chocolate. The cola tree provides nuts that flavor certain well-known soft drinks.

Dombeya wallichii • **hydrangea tree, African mallow**

The coral-pink or red flowers of the hydrangea tree form massive, ball-shaped, drooping clusters about three inches across. In Hawai'i the trees tend to bloom in the fall and winter, but the blossoms hang on the tree long after they've turned brown. This is a

small tree sometimes grown as a large shrub. The broad, toothed leaves grow up to a foot long. They are sharply veined above, hairy underneath and along the long leaf-stems. This purely ornamental tree originated in Madagascar.

Clusiaceae

The mangosteen family is a small group (about one thousand species) widely distributed in tropical regions.

Calophyllum inophyllum • **kamani**

The Polynesians brought this good-looking seashore tree to Hawai'i. The shiny, stiff, dark-green leaves, about eight inches long, are oval or elliptical in shape with a slightly notched tip. The fragrant white flowers are organized in multiples of four. Fruits look like cherries, but with a thin yellow or brown pulp and a large round seed. The seed

provides a dark green oil used medicinally or as an ointment. Kamani belongs to the class of island hardwoods that both was and is the focus of the woodworkers' art. Its sapwood is white and its heartwood is red. The tree resists salt spray and flourishes in places as remote as Hālawa Valley, Moloka'i, and the Puna district, Hawai'i. It also graces many of O'ahu's streets, for example Dillingham Boulevard and roads near the Dole Pineapple Cannery.

Clusia rosea • **autograph tree**

Large, thick, shiny, red-veined leaves give this tree its main appeal as a handsome ornamental. These unusual leaves are "obovate"—that is, oval but narrowest at the stem end and broadest at the tip. And they get to be eight inches long in both directions. Leaves are so dense that you can scratch designs or words onto them. In fact, you will often see this in Hawai'i—clusia trees on which people have appeased their desire to leave Kilroy-was-here type messages. Hence the common name. In the same way, people in this tree's native West Indies used to make

the leaves into playing cards. *Clusia rosea* bears two-inch-diameter white or pink flowers followed by round, greenish-brown fruit capsules three inches across. Because it tolerates salt spray, the tree is often grown in coastal areas.

Bixaceae

The annatto family of tropical America is so small as to contain only one genus with two species. If it weren't for the annatto dye plant, this family would hardly exist, let alone be famous.

Bixa orellana • **lipstick tree, annatto dye plant**

Natives of South America discovered long ago that they could paint their bodies with the scarlet, lipstick-like coating on the seeds of *Bixa orellana*. Scientists in more recent times discovered that this same coating yields a yellow or red dye with nutritional value. For a while, this dye, called annatto or arnotto, was used extensively to color food (butter, cheese, candy, chocolate) and to make soap and paint. Now synthetic dyes have taken over, but the appeal of annatto served to give this medium-size tree a wide circulation. Hawaiians have another name for the lipstick tree—'alaea, their term for the red earth that they used (rather similarly) as a dye. The leaves of lipstick tree are long-stemmed, oval or heart-shaped, and as long as seven inches. Flowers look like wild roses, pink or white. The softly spiked seed capsules develop in fat clusters at the branch-tips, starting out red then turning brown before splitting open to reveal the unusual seeds.

Caricaceae

The papaya group is a very small tropical family with an eccentric style all its own.

Carica papaya • **papaya**

In terms of what people usually consider a "tree," the papaya stretches the definition. Unbranching (usually), the plants shoot quickly to heights anywhere from five to twenty-five feet. All the foliage is clustered in a single daffy-looking spray at the top, with the fruit clustered tight against the trunk below this. There is no wood in the tree; rather, the trunk is hollow and held together by tough fibers in the bark. (These fibers are strong enough to be fashioned into rope.) The "trees" are short-lived, usually expiring after fewer than ten years. But what productive years those are! Plants yield, nonstop, pounds of what is arguably Hawai'i's most popular homegrown fruit. The papaya fruit is oval, usually about six inches long, and heavy with yellow, orange, or somewhat reddish meat. The central cavity is full of small hard

black seeds, each one covered with a smooth skin and gelatinous coat. The fruit, eaten raw or cooked in stews, provides an excellent source of vitamins and calcium. The seeds have a mustard flavor and are thought to be medicinal. (It's customary in Hawai'i to leave one seed in each half-fruit serving.) Also, the fruit and leaves contain the enzyme papain, so both are used to tenderize meat. Most varieties of papaya are hermaphroditic, meaning that male and female flowers occur on the same, self-pollinating plant. But certain varieties retain this plant's ancestral two-sex habit—some are male, others female. In this case, a male needs to be present to stimulate fruit in the others. Male trees are obvious for their lack of fruit and for their spikes of white flowers that shoot and branch out of the treetop.

(ABOVE) papaya fruit
(BELOW) flowers of a male papaya

Rhizophoraceae

Most of the hundred species of this tropical family exercise the odd mangrove ability to grow in marsh and tidewater.

Rhizophora mangle • **mangrove**

The mangrove thrives in an impossibly toxic situation—seaside marshes, where it roots in saltwater or brackish water. To keep from drowning, this plant develops stilt roots that stay above the water line. These aerial roots curve and arch, forming a dense thicket. In this way, a mass of mangroves will actually hold a shoreline against the action of water, collecting silt and building soil. In fact, that's why Hawai'i has mangroves at all. (This type of mangrove comes from the tropical Atlantic shores of the New World.) The American Sugar

Paul Wood

Company introduced them in 1902 to stabilize the mud flats of southwest Moloka'i. Now you can find them on that island and on Kaua'i, O'ahu (the shoreline reefs at Kāne'ohe Bay, for example), Lāna'i, and Hawai'i. The trees flower and fruit year-round. The fruit clings to the twig and develops a seedling that hangs from it like a thin cigar. Eventually these heavy seedlings fall to the mud, where they may drift in the currents till they find a new place to root.

Paul Wood

Combretaceae

The "tropical almond" family comprises four hundred species of tropical trees and shrubs.

Terminalia catappa • **tropical almond, false kamani**

This salt-tolerant seashore tree from the East Indies is widely planted around the world, mainly because it is hardy and attractive. It was introduced to Hawai'i, and it naturalized, in the early years of European contact. Leaves are broad, shiny, and almost a foot long. A strong identifying feature is the bright red color that the old leaves take on before they fall. These trees also produce a distinctive fruit almost year-round—an oval, lens-shaped nut in a fleshy skin. The slightly sour skin is edible; so is the nut, which cracks open rather like an almond. (Hence

the common name, "tropical almond.") The term "false kamani" is rather unfortunate, as there is nothing treacherous about this fine tree. But this plant looks somewhat similar to the native kamani and grows in the same habitat. Its wood is sometimes used in craftwork as a substitute for kamani, but it is less beautiful and less durable.

Paul Wood

Myrtaceae

The myrtle family has been a great source of trees for Hawai'i. Besides the eucalypts, the family includes several tropical fruit trees and an endemic tree of great significance. All of these bear brushy-looking flowers with petals absent or minute.

Eucalyptus spp. • **eucalyptus**

Over ninety species of this successful, mostly Australian genus have been introduced to Hawaiian forests. At least one-third of them have naturalized to some extent. As a group, the eucalypts grow quickly and reach great heights. In fact, these are the world's tallest hardwood trees, some topping three hundred feet. Foliage is typically aromatic and resinous. The trunks of some species yield a gum or resin. The brushy flowers form inside a woody capsule, emerging after a distinctive "lid" (operculum) pops off and falls to the ground.

Eucalyptus citriodora • **lemon-gum eucalyptus**

This eucalyptus can be recognized by the strong lemon odor that arises from its crushed foliage or that simply wafts in the air on a sunny day. Other key features: the long, narrow leaves that form a thin, open crown, and the smooth gray bark that peels in irregular patches. Seed capsules are egg-shaped. In Hawai'i the lemon-gum prefers lower elevations, where it attains a height of one hundred feet or more. On O'ahu you can find an avenue of these trees at the entrance to 'Ualaka'a Park (Round Top), and it is the main tree bordering Wahiawā Reservoir.

(LEFT) lemon-gum eucalyptus

Eucalyptus deglupta • **rainbow eucalyptus**

People stare in fascination at the trunks of these smooth-barked trees. As the outer bark falls away, it reveals strips and layers of bright contrasting colors—green, pink, yellow, red, orange, even purple. Native to the Philippines and Indonesia, *Eucalyptus deglupta* was planted extensively on most islands during the 1940s. "Rainbow eucalyptus" seems to be a local island term. Elsewhere these trees are called Bagras eucalyptus and Mindanao gum. One of the world's fastest-growing trees, it has been known to reach one hundred feet tall in seven years.

85

Eucalyptus robusta • **swamp mahogany**

At one time, *Eucalyptus robusta*
was the most commonly planted
tree in Hawai'i—nearly five million planted before 1960. Its massive trunk is swathed with thick,
soft, spongy, reddish brown bark.
Leaves are broadly lance-shaped;
seed capsules are large and bell-
shaped. Its wood, as with most
eucalypts, can be difficult to mill,
as it tends to split and spring. And
yet lumber from *Eucalyptus robusta*
has been used for pallets, stakes,
and rough framing purposes.

Eugenia uniflora • **Surinam cherry**

This robust shrub grows to the size
and shape of a small tree, up to
twenty feet tall and wide. Juicy red
fruit about the size of a small cherry tomato forms with a distinctive
pleated look. The taste is spicy-tart,
sometimes rather sweet. The fruit
lends itself well to preserves. This
species originated in Brazil, but
people have carried Surinam cherry
all over the globe—no doubt
because it provides fruit so readily
but also because it is such a
healthy looking plant, rich with

shiny leaves reminiscent of myrtle and boxwood. It came to Hawai'i about 1870. Now you find it growing wild in moist lowland areas on all the main islands. This close relative of Hawai'i's 'ōhi'a lehua and mountain apple shares the same genus with another famous plant, one cultivated for its spicy flower buds—the clove tree.

Melaleuca quinquenervia • **paperbark, cajeput tree**

This hardy, fast-growing Australian tree has been widely planted in Hawai'i's forest preserves. In fact, with 1.7 million introductions, this is the third most commonly planted tree in the islands. It serves as a watershed cover and windbreak, but it is also ornamental. Its distinguishing feature is its unusual bark—thick, whitish, spongy, and peeling away in countless paper-like layers. Leaves are narrow, light green, and (as with the related

87

eucalypts) give off a resinous odor. Flowers form white "bottlebrushes" at the twig-tips. The small seed capsules cling to the older wood like so many barnacles. The bark has been used elsewhere for packing material, boat caulking, and torches, and the cajeput oil of medicine is steam-distilled from the leaves and twigs. In Hawai'i, however, the paperbark tree has not been put to much use.

Metrosideros polymorpha • 'ōhi'a lehua

If one had to select a signature endemic species to represent the strange and vigorous beauty of Hawai'i's native flora, certainly one would choose 'ōhi'a lehua—or, as most people put it, "the ohia tree." (Pronounced o-HEE-ah.) The most common native tree in the islands, it grows from sea level to timberline in wet and dry forests. This plant is extremely variable in leaf shape, hairiness, flower color, and stature. (Hence the species name polymorpha, which means "many shapes.") In some situations it will grow to eighty or even one hundred feet tall with three-foot-diameter trunks. Elsewhere, it's no more than a creeping shrub. Most people think of the red-flowered form, the official flower of Hawai'i island, but pink, salmon, and yellow forms exist. Considering the flowers sacred to Pele, the goddess of fire, Hawaiians weave them into lei and speak of them in chants and

(RIGHT) 'ōhi'a lehua

legends. Many types of native birds feed on their nectar. Hawaiians used the heavy wood for construction and household implements. Modern uses have included flooring, marine construction, fenceposts, and 'ukulele keys. The Santa Fe Railroad Company once used five million railroad ties made of 'ōhi'a lehua. Now, fortunately for Hawai'i, these important natives are not much harvested.

Pimenta dioica • **allspice**

The name "allspice" refers to this tree's small but powerfully aromatic berries. Picked green and dried, these berries have the combined flavors of clove, nutmeg, and cinnamon, and so are used for cooking and for making perfume. The foliage releases the same spicy smell, especially when crushed. Allspice is a medium-size tree (twenty to forty feet), very handsome with its smooth, leathery, lance-shaped leaves that grow up to six inches long. Leaves are almost stemless, so the tree has a dense, robust look to it. The tree is native to the West Indies. Jamaica, for example, exports thousands of tons of allspice each year.

Psidium cattleianum • **strawberry guava, waiawā**

This small, shiny-leafed tree was introduced to Hawai'i for its tasty fruits. These are round berries an inch or so across with red or sometimes yellow skin, white tangy pulp, and numerous small seeds. People eat them fresh and make them into jam or punch. The bark of this tree is smooth and light brown, peeling away to reveal a green layer underneath. The wood makes excellent fire fuel. Because the stems are so hard and straight, people cut them to make walking sticks. This would be quite a commendable little tree were it not such a pest. Pigs and birds do an excellent job of scattering its seeds, and other plants have difficulty establishing themselves where strawberry guava has intruded.

Psidium guajava • **guava**

Similar in most ways to the strawberry guava—including its tendency to intrude on wild landscapes—the common guava offers a large yellow berry up to three inches across. The pulp is pink. Unusually high in vitamin C, the fruit is processed and sold as a zesty juice. It also makes good jam, paste, and preserves, and of course it's eaten raw although the numerous beebee-like seeds have to be spit out or swallowed. Boys will tell you that guava branches are perfect for making slingshots—the

hard, slender wood forms crotches of just the right angle. Leaves are pale green, up to four inches long, and creased with strong veins. Guava spreads aggressively by both seed and root sprouts. It came to Hawai'i in the early 1800s, and by 1871 it had already begun to squeeze other plant life out of the valleys. The fallen fruit makes a marvelous breeding ground for fruit flies.

Syzygium malaccensis • **mountain apple, 'ōhi'a 'ai**

Early Polynesian settlers brought the mountain apple to Hawai'i. It is similar to its cousin the rose apple in several ways: lance-shaped, dark leaves, flowers that look like a brush of long stamens, and a tendency to naturalize in moist areas. But mountain apple tops the other in stature (fifty feet or more) and in quality of fruit. The fruits really do look and taste like small apples with purple-red (sometimes whitish) skin and white, crisp flesh. In spring when the trees bloom, they will drop a carpet of purple-red stamens on the forest floor—an

eye-catching sight. Besides eating the fruit, the Hawaiians fashioned the wood into posts, rafters, and fences, carved it into religious images, and relieved sore throats with a tea brewed from its bark. In 1793 Captain William Bligh brought mountain apples to Jamaica along with breadfruit trees, hoping to establish a cheap food source for slaves.

Araliaceae

The ginseng family, a mainly tropical bunch, includes panax shrubs, English ivy, and thirteen species of endemic Hawaiian trees (now scarce).

Schefflera actinophylla • **octopus tree**

Familiar to indoor gardeners as a potted plant, the octopus tree grows to its full potential—twenty to forty feet—in Hawai'i's benign climate. The leaves are distinctive: seven to twelve large oval leaflets on long stalks radiating, umbrella-like, from a single point. The long flower stalks likewise radiate from a single point, ten to twenty of them fanning out from the branch tips. These flower stalks are dark purple with red or crimson flowers. They look something like octopus tentacles, hence the common name. The blue-black berries will

stain sidewalks. Trees form several unbranched trunks and seem to do well with relatively few leaves. Introduced to Hawai'i around 1900, the octopus tree has escaped and become something of a pest. One of its tricks: seeds will germinate in other trees and send roots down to the ground.

Loganiaceae

This widespread and diverse family has made few contributions to horticulture. However, the genus *Strychnos* provides all sorts of poisons and strong medicines, among them being strychnine and the blow-gun poison curare.

Fagraea berteriana • **puakenikeni**

The large, succulent, trumpet-shaped flowers of puakenikeni fade from cream to orange, all the while emitting a delicious fragrance. They are most highly prized for lei and for perfuming coconut oil. Native to the South Pacific, the puakenikeni tree plays a sacred role in legends of Polynesia. Tahitians carved its wood into images of Tane, god of the forests.

Paul Wood

Paul Wood

The Hawaiian name means "ten-cent flower" because the flowers used to be sold for the phenomenal price of a dime apiece. Trees can grow to forty feet, though they are often kept shrub-high. Leaves are attractive and shiny, about six inches long and three inches wide. Birds love the inch-long berries, which are orange or red.

Apocynaceae

A mid-size tropical group of great variety, the periwinkle family contributed eight species to Hawai'i's native flora, including the maile vine used for lei and the lovely but now rare holei trees.

Plumeria acuminata • **yellow plumeria**
Plumeria obtusa • **white plumeria**
Plumeria rubra • **red plumeria**

The plumeria, also called frangipani, produces great quantities of Hawai'i's most reliable and popular lei flower. Borne in clusters on the stem-ends, these five-parted flowers about two inches across possess a spongy durability and a delightful fragrance. The long floral tube seems perfectly designed to accept the lei-maker's needle. When snapped from the stem, flowers release a drop of sticky white sap. In fact, the entire tree, especially the thick succulent branches, is loaded with this latex,

which is poisonous. Leaves are oblong, pointed at each end, and large—up to sixteen inches long. On most plumeria, leaves fall from the tree in winter and return after blooming begins in spring. These are small, broad-spreading trees native to tropical America. The flowers of *Plumeria acuminata* are predominately yellow, those of *Plumeria obtusa* are white with a yellow throat, and those of *Plumeria rubra* are rose, red, or wine-colored. Hybrids express countless variations.

95

Boraginaceae

Most members of the widespread heliotrope family are small herbs or shrubs. A typical characteristic of this group is the fiddleneck look of the flower clusters, which usually unroll in the manner of a scorpion's tail.

Cordia sebestena • **kou haole**

Called "haole" (foreign) because it is an ornamental tree of recent introduction, this species of *Cordia* bears bright orange flowers nearly all year round. Leaves are rich dark green, oval, up to eight inches long. Flowers are crepe-like and frilled, one to two inches across. The small white fruit is edible. These are small evergreen trees that originated in the West Indies.

Cordia subcordata • **kou**

A small broad-crowned tree with showy light-orange flowers, kou came to Hawai'i with the early Polynesians. Unlike many of the so-called "canoe plants," kou did not naturalize much, and even in the dry coastal areas favored by this plant it is not common. The Hawaiians cultivated kou primarily for its wood, which they favored for making bowls and utensils. Kou wood is attractive, easy to work, and free of any flavors that might pass into the food. Flowers are funnel-shaped and well over an inch wide. Leaves are thin, broadly oval, up to seven inches long. The seeds are edible.

Tournefortia argentea • **tree heliotrope**

This distinctive beach tree originated around the Indian Ocean and has naturalized along the shorelines of all major Hawaiian islands. It is small and umbrella-shaped, reaching twenty feet high and forty feet wide. Leaves are fuzzy and gray-green, wider toward the tip than at the base. Flower and fruit clusters form in tightly packed, curling rows. Flowers are tiny and white, consisting of five spreading, rounded lobes. Leaves have a salty taste. People in India eat them raw.

Bignoniaceae

This primarily tropical family expresses itself with long, bright-colored, trumpet-shaped flowers. Its members include many brilliant vines and the gorgeous flowering trees shown here.

Crescentia cujete • **calabash tree**

This is a low, short-trunked tree with long spreading or drooping branches. Leaves arrange themselves spirally around the branches,

sometimes in tufts. The main attraction, of course, is the bowling-ball-shaped fruit, which swells up to a foot in diameter. This fruit consists of pulp and seeds inside a hard shell, which can be carved and polished. The tree comes from Mexico, where people tie the unripe fruits to force them into various shapes, then harvest them for use as bowls and ornaments. In Hawai'i they get made into hula rattles, somewhat substituting for the native ipu or gourd.

Jacaranda mimosifolia • **jacaranda**

Lavender-blue trees are the stuff of fantasy. So when the jacaranda lets go each spring—its delicate fern-like leaves having all fallen—and covers itself with purplish trumpets, the mind reels. When it carpets the lawn below with cast-off

blooms, the color-contrast dazzles one's vision. These South America natives form a rounded crown up to fifty feet high. Seedpods are round, woody capsules, something like flat brown clams or hefty potato chips. The jacaranda was introduced to Hawai'i around 1900 and has naturalized on the islands of O'ahu, Maui, and Hawai'i.

Spathodea campanulata • **African tulip tree**

Brilliant orange-red flower clusters flash boldly at the top of this dark-leaved shade tree. Because *Spathodea* reproduces easily both from seed and root sprout, this handsome tree has become fully naturalized. It is often seen in wild places blending its bright color with the like of kukui and koa trees. This is a large tree, to eighty feet tall,

with a big trunk supported by tall narrow buttresses at the base. Narrow lance-shaped pods can be ten inches long, splitting open along one side to release hordes of papery, wind-scattered seeds. This native of West Africa is widely planted in tropical regions around the world. The flower buds are full of stinky water that squirts out when the buds are squeezed; kids like to use them as water pistols.

Rubiaceae

The coffee and gardenia family includes numerous shrubs of great ornamental value. One member is a tree of exotic significance from ancient Hawaiian times.

Morinda citrifolia • **Indian mulberry, noni**

The early Hawaiians brought this small (twenty feet) Asian tree to the islands, apparently for its cure-all qualities. Leaves are broad, shiny green, up to a foot long, with sunken, curved veins. The small white flowers are crowded into spherical clusters, which then develop into odd, fleshy fruits covered with lumpy "eyeballs." As this fruit ripens and softens, it turns a

translucent white and gives off a fetid, cheese-like odor. Whole books have been written about the curative qualities of this stinky fruit, and noni juice is sold commercially as a health supplement. In fact, all parts of this tree are used in folk remedies. A poultice of the leaves will alleviate pain. The Hawaiians extracted dyes for their kapa cloth from noni—red from the bark and yellow from the trunk and roots.

Where to See Hawai'i's Trees

The US Department of Agriculture Forest Service identifies the following twenty "Special Areas" for best viewing of Hawai'i's magnificent trees:

Hawai'i

1 Pu'uhonua o Hōnaunau National
   Historical Park (City of Refuge)
2 Hawai'i Volcanoes National Park
3 Kalōpā State Park
4 KīpukaPuaulu (Bird Park) Trail
5 Pepe'ekeo Arboretum
6 Waiākea Arboretum

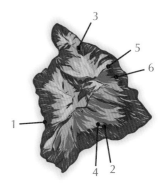

Kaua'i

1 Keāhua Forestry Arboretum
2 Kōke'e State Park, especially along Awa'awapuhi Trail
3 Pacific Tropical Botanical Garden in Lāwa'i

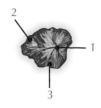

Maui

1 Haleakalā National Park
2 Kula Botanical Garden
3 Kula Forest Reserve (Poli Poli Spring)
4 Waihou Spring Forest Reserve (Olinda)

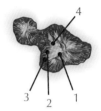

O'ahu

1 'Aiea Loop Trail
2 Foster Botanic Garden in Honolulu
3 'Iolani Palace grounds, Honolulu
4 Koko Crater Botanic Garden
5 Tantalus Round Top Drive
6 Wahiawā Botanic Garden
7 Waimea Valley Audubon Center

African tulip tree • 100
Spathodea campanulata

allspice • 90
Pimenta dioica

'ama'u • 17
Sadleria cyatheoides

autograph tree • 77
Clusia rosea

avocado • 46
Persea americana

banana • 29
Musa x paradisiaca

bottle palm • 26
Mascarena lagenicaulis

breadfruit • 34
Artocarpus altilis
'ulu

calabash tree • 99
Crescentia cujete

camphor • 45
Cinnamomum camphora

candlenut • 65
Aleurites moluccana
kukui

cherimoya • 44
Annona cherimola

Chinese banyan • 39
Ficus microcarpa

Christmas-berry • 69
Schinus terebinthifolia

coconut • 25
Cocos nucifera
niu

common bamboo • 24
Bambusa vulgaris
'ohe

Cook pine • 19
Araucaria columnaris

coral trees • 57
Erythrina spp.

cycad • 18
Cycas circinalis
Sago palm

dragon tree • 28
Dracaena draco

eucalyptus • 83
Eucalyptus spp.

fern tree • 70
Filicium decipiens

figs • 37

guava • 91
Psidium guajava

hala • 23
Pandanus tectorius

hāpu'u • 16
Cibotium chamissoi

hau • 73
Hibiscus tileaceus

Hong Kong orchid tree • 52
Bauhinia blakeana

hydrangea tree • 75
Dombeya wallichii
African mallow

Indian banyan • 38
Ficus benghalensis

Indian mulberry • 101
Morinda citrifolia
noni

ironwood • 33
Casuarina glauca
Casuarina

Italian cypress • 21
Cupressus sempervirens

jacaranda • 99
Jacaranda mimosifolia

jack fruit • 36
Artocarpus heterophyllus

kamani • 76
Calophyllum inophyllum

kiawe • 62
Prosopis pallida

koa • 49
Acacia koa

kou • 97
Cordia subcordata

kou haole • 96
Cordia sebestena

lemon-gum eucalyptus • 85
Eucalyptus citriodora

lipstick tree • 78
Bixa orellana
annatto dye plant

litchi • 71
Litchi chinensis
lychee

loquat • 47
Eriobotrya japonica

macadamia • 41
Macadamia integrifolia

mango • 67
Mangifera indica

mangrove • 81
Rhizophora mangle

milo • 74
Thespesia populnea

monkeypod • 60
Pithecellobium saman

mountain apple • 92
Syzygium malaccensis
'ōhi'a 'ai

Norfolk Island pine • 20
Araucaria heterophylla

octopus tree • 93
Schefflera actinophylla

'ōhi'a lehua • 88
Metrosideros polymorpha

'opiuma • 58
Pithecellobium dulce

papaya • 79
Carica papaya

paperbark • 87
Melaleuca quinquenervia
cajeput tree

pepper tree • 68
Schinus molle

pink bauhinia • 52
Bauhinia monandra
St. Thomas tree

plumeria • 95
Plumeria acuminata

puakenikeni • 94
berteriana

rainbow eucalyptus • 85
Eucalyptus deglupta

red plumeria • 95
Plumeria rubra

royal palm • 26
Roystonea regia

royal poinciana • 54
Delonix regia

rubber tree • 38
Ficus elastica

sea grape • 43
Coccoloba uvifera

shower trees • 53
Cassia spp.

silk oak • 40
Grevillea robusta

strawberry guava • 91
Psidium cattleianum
waiawā

Surinam cherry • 86
Eugenia uniflora

swamp mahogany • 86
Eucalyptus robusta

tamarind • 64
Tamarindus indica

travelers palm • 31
Ravenala madagascariensis

tree heliotrope • 98
Tournefortia argentea

tropical almond • 82
Terminalia catappa
false kamani

wattle • 50
Acacia mearnsii
black-wattle acacia

wiliwili • 56
Erythrina sandwicense

Paul Wood had the fortune in youth to apprentice with an extraordinary naturalist—Oscar C. Clarke, long-time curator of the herbarium at University of California Riverside. He worked as Oscar Clarke's herbarium assistant, then carried his passion for botany into a couple of mid-twenties gigs—as a nurseryman (California certified) and as a landscape contractor. In time, he got re-focused on his abiding work as a writer and writing teacher. Now, after twenty-five years in Hawai'i, this book has given him the opportunity to pull a few threads together.

Other books written by Paul Wood include:
Proteas and *Flowers and Plants of Hawai'i.*

Ron Dahlquist sold his first picture to a small surfing publication almost thirty years ago. Today he is a nationally acclaimed photographer whose repertoire ranges from action sports to sensitive pictures of the environment and worldwide travel. His images have appeared in such publications as *Life, Time, National Geographic, World, Forbes, Esquire, Islands, Condé Nast Traveler, Vanity Fair, Outside, Ski, Surfer's Journal, Snowboarder,* and *Windsurfer.* His coffee table book *Under a Maui Sun* was released at the end of 2000.

Art prints from the photography in this book are available by contacting www.rondahlquist.com.